Burning the Fence

Burning the Fence

Walter McDonald

Texas Tech Press
Lubbock, Texas, U.S.A.
1981

Also by Walter McDonald

Caliban in Blue
  Voertman's Poetry Award,
  The Texas Institute of Letters

One Thing Leads to Another (chapbook)

Anything, Anything

Working Against Time (chapbook)

ISBN 0-89672-987-X (paper)
ISBN 0-89672-088-8 (cloth)
Library of Congress Catalog Number:80-54792

Designed by Joyce S. Pollard, set in Hanover,
printed on Texas Tech Opaque, 70 lb.
Cover and dust jacket design based on a
photograph by James Broderick

Texas Tech Press
Texas Tech University
Lubbock, Texas 79409
Copyright 1981 by Texas Tech University
Printed in the United States of America

Acknowledgments

Grateful acknowledgment is made to the following publications for poems, some in earlier versions, which appeared in them.

Ascent: "The Lifeguard"
Aura: "First Blood," "The Winter Before the War"
The CEA Critic: "Evolution," "Sangre de Cristo, September 6," "The White-Haired Trial Judge Deliberates"
Cedar Rock: "After Years in the Mountains"
Christmas in Texas (Brown Rabbit Press): "Scouting Arapaho"
English in Texas: "Llano Estacado"
Hiram Poetry Review: "Tornado Alley"
The Keeper of Juno's Swans (Baylor University Press): "Claiming Kin," "The Corner Grocery Store," "Going Home," "Morning in Texas"
The Limberlost Review: "Snow Takes Us"
Moons & Lion Tailes: "Last Words to an Apprentice Undertaker"
The New York Quarterly: "Al Croom"
One Thing Leads to Another (Cedar Rock Press): "We Three"
The Pawn Review: "Measuring Time"
Phantasm: "Taking Aim"
raccoon 4: "Oases"
Re: Artes Liberales: "Veteran"
riverSedge: "Something of Me Reminds You of Fog"
Rocky Mountain Review: "Near Durango, July 18," "Never in My Life"
Sam Houston Literary Review: "Weekends"
Sands: "First Solo"
The Sound of a Few Leaves (The Rook Press): "Burning the Fence"
The Spoon River Quarterly: "The End of Summer," "University Library"
Vision: "Bermuda Grass," "With Steve at Lake Raven"
Working Against Time (The Calliope Press): "Weekends," "With Steve at Lake Raven"
Writers Forum 6: "World War I Soldiers"

Burning the Fence

Contents

I

Morning in Texas

Early afternoon
April-hot, sticky, no wind,
windows open in Miss James' class.
The boom like a bomb,
then softer crashes,
concrete chunks big as doors
smashing houses
near the grain elevator.

Juan Hernandez, whose father
worked inside the elevator hold,
jumped straight up
burst the desk top
shouted My papa oh
my papa's dead!

That night mother told me
Just a coincidence,
Juan couldn't have known.
She pulled the sheet up over my arms.
I said Mother, I'm going to die.

All night I lay there
starting to explode,
feeling my spirit crouched,
ready to burst
from my splattered body.
Dawn came. Comes.

Billy Bastard and the Centipede

Bastrop was his name. We called him
Billy Bastard. He cut window screens,
tied cats' tails together with string,
set fire to the garage next door.

He stole a scalpel, tweezers, alcohol.
We crowded around his specimens
pickled in jars: grasshoppers, garter snakes,
a tarantula floating like a baby octopus.

Once he caught a centipede ten inches long,
dangled it over a jar of alcohol.
Took out the scalpel, cut off several legs.
Wiggling, it crawled away.

He tweezered it and sliced off more.
Put down, the creature still could crawl.
You stop it, Billy Bastard, some girl said.
His mouth cupped the slightest grin.

He shaved away more legs, dark like eyelashes.
I'll tell, that girl warned, and began to cry.
Each time he let it down,
it dragged its back-half like a sled.

He sliced the last.
It writhed, rolled over
on its twitching stumps.
Some of us stayed, looked on.

He sliced it like sausage piece by piece
till all that lived were stumps,
a head, two eyes that bulged,
that took each of us in.

Plowing through Ashes

After frost, grain-sorghum stubble
yellow as wheat
hid pairs of pheasants
scattered on the plains.
Seven, eight times a season
we searched the rows,
shotguns stiff, dogs sniffing ahead,
and took our necessary meat.

After the last snow
we torched the stalks,
the orange flames
spreading like a prairie fire,
covering the fields with soot.

March, after the dirt cooled,
my father plowed the charred
earth brown again,
like flipping a reversible jacket
seam by seam.
Unless it rained, he ditched,
for two weeks irrigated,
and in May
he rigged the tractor up,
lowered four worn plows
into the ground
and planted grain.

University Library

Banyan and bougainvillea sprawl in the foyer,
fountains splash syllables of sleep.
Students in far corners stretch out together,
smoking, the exit bar clicking
each time someone leaves. At card catalogs
librarians index astounding bound books
from everywhere. The elevator is packed
with people of all ages going up, going down.

Deep in the stacks in fourth floor
carrels, graduate males massage
slide rules backwards and forwards,
mastering bodies of knowledge
by degrees and dreaming beyond facts
of the inscrutable design of young wives.

Cabin

If we build here
all sorts of things are possible:
dawn earlier, fog curled at our feet,
the spring far enough downhill
for exercise, buckets of water
balanced for the cool climb home.

Here's where from down below
we've seen elk silhouetted,
here we'll be level with hawks
perched high in the piñon,
look, one's watching us, swaying,
its dark eyes blinking.

Up here, the breeze will be
always strong, the chimney will draw,
the roof swirled free of snow,
and in spring we'll dust,
shake blankets fresh outside,
and beat the rugs.

Scouting Arapaho

to my sons

You can't believe it's this cold,
that you're here alone. Snow
slopes two feet up the tent.
Breakfast, bouillon and spam,
warm up together on the gerry stove.
Only the fact you pitched your tent
eastward locates the sun,
buried by clouds. Two more nights
of shivering and sweating
in a goose-down bag,
three days to earn a badge.
Fed, you strap on new
snow shoes and start to stalk
rabbits, ermine, anything
for pictures to prove
you didn't hibernate.
At a stream
you clear the ice of snow.
Something, a flash
of fish, waves too fast
to photograph, colors
so soft they melt away.
You come back later in the day,
and clear more snow, and skate.

Near Durango, July 18

The warning flags are up:
No fires. No fires.
Pumas and mule deer stand
on three feet. They move
cautiously over dry rocks
down to the shallow stream
bumping its way
from boulder
to boulder.
They sniff the air,
then drink.
The trees smell brittle;
the shrubs, of dust.
In the clear sky
buzzards patrol the woods.
The hot air rising
holds them aloft for hours.
Heat waves shimmer
like bleached rainbows.
The forest waits
to ignite.

After Years in the Mountains

we've come back to the plains.
What for. To ease our parents'
last years. To be with friends
who never left. To take a job.

In Colorado we had four seasons,
real snow, always other rocks to see,
trails leading nowhere we thought
but wilderness. We tried

to get lost. Always we found
another trail or others like us
packing in, climbing for Eden.
And now we live on the plains,

the sky so wide it startled us
our first day here. Our children,
used to the walls of mountains,
run as if they've been set free.

They make new friends,
begin to play, learn how
to breathe this thicker air.
We rise earlier, watch the sun

pull itself over the plains,
and at night we watch it setting
far away. In the mountains
we had nighttime sooner.

Here there are no mosquitoes,
no snakes, no deer in the clearing
at dusk. Something has been lost.
Some things remain.

We hold each other
a long while,
unload another box,
and start to settle in.

Llano Estacado

Comanches crossed these plains
tracking buffalo. Now, when our eyes
burst with boredom, we ride an hour
across a trail of asphalt
through cotton fields flat as our lawn
and park at the caprock.

The staked plains stop
like the delta of a lava flow:
below, far to the east,
sagebrush on rocky slopes,
cairns fifty feet high,
gullies and thin plateaus.

Buzzards in level circles
prowl the sky, tracking
all sorts of life: coons,
coyotes, armadillos and skunks,
porcupines and snakes,
rabbits with round eyes
and rapidly beating hearts.

Tornado Alley

Each spring before the thunderstorms begin
we lift the flat steel door and climb down steps
so steep we bump the wall for balance.
I jerk the string, light sprays the cellar floor.
Spiders dark as funnel clouds swirl themselves down
and swivel into cracks. Lawn chairs webbed with dust
lean on the walls. We find a book missing all winter,
dominoes still stacked from last year's last alert.

We lug the chairs outside, dust and sweep up,
test flashlight batteries, refill the water jug.
The dominoes go back inside their box.
Dusted, lawn chairs go back against the walls.
We prop the steel door wide to ventilate.
We search the sky. There's time.

II

First Blood

I saw a plane crash
when I was ten.
Walking with Nolan
I heard the roar
then saw it zoom up
to its left and level off.
It circled and began to dive.
We hit each other.
The nose burst up so steep
it almost ripped our eyes.
We saw it circle
then nose-down
and dive again.
We saw it clip the wires
and crash.
I don't know what we said.
We got up off the ground,
we saw the tail so still,
no sound, sticking up
out of the house.
Nothing caught fire. Neighbors
poured out from all around,
came screaming, wringing
their hands. Somebody said
this guy was buzzing Shirley,
he used to go with her.
She wasn't home.
Nolan and I were late
for school. Each of us
took a piece of the plane.
Mine had some blood on it.

The Corner Grocery Store

Slope-shouldered, thin,
disabled by the Bataan
death march,
my boss sold
whatever he could stock
on meager shelves

in 1946. Mornings
after fits of coughing
he scouted ads,
sent me for specials
to what in ten years more
they'd call the supermarkets.

Shaking his head
he marked each item up
however much he thought
would sell.
Once a day
he called his ex-wife

long distance, ended
slamming the phone down,
screaming at me.
Always his crotch
itched from jungle rot.
Halfway through a sale

he'd motion me to ring it up
and rush out scratching wildly.
He had a trunk of souvenirs,
Japanese coins and teeth
and paper bills thick
as parchment. He doled them out,

bribed me to settle
for fifty cents a day.
Within six months his souvenirs,
his jungle rot, his customers
that never bought
more than a dollar's worth,

drove him to bed,
wheezing for me to ring
exactly what they bought,
called me thief, one morning
hissed *You Jap*
you murderer get out.

First Solo

When you break ground, let the sky take you,
lifting you into nothing but air.
It is not a swing, you will not fall back.
Retract the wheels like a crane tucking up its legs
for flight. Turning crosswind you may
glance at the ground, but try not to stare
at sunlight skimming across the ponds
and bridges. If you look too long, the nose
will drop in the turn. Remember Lot's wife.

Crosscheck your airspeed often, obey the needle
as you would your god. If you ignore it
you may stall. Somewhere in your mind
you will dream of choking. It will be your own hand
squeezing the controls. Relax, you are suspending
no one over a cliff. The wings will hold you up,
if you remember airspeed.

On downwind, level off. Notice the runway
beneath your wing. For a time you will know
you are alone, and flying. Soon you must drop
the wheels down into place. Check that they lock.
When the runway disappears beneath your wing,
make yourself fly on for seconds. Though they seem
like hours, you will not be lost. At last

when you see the runway's end behind your wing,
it will be time to turn. Ease back the throttle,
and begin to fall. Roll out on final approach
and glide toward the runway. And check your airspeed.

If you stall, there's no time to recover. The runway,
keep thinking the runway. Something inside
will aim you down. As you cross the end, raise the nose,
hold off, off, and cut the power.
Give everything you have to the runway.
You will have all night to dream.

Claiming Kin

My uncle Edward flew
for the Lafayette Escadrille,
drank his way all over Europe,
hitched home to Texas in '21,
sired three sons,
barnstormed around the South,
the North, and Canada. In '23
went fifteen rounds with Tunney,
Tunney never knocked him down,
broke my uncle Edward's nose.
His wife remarried
when he was off somewhere.
In '45 he settled down
in Dallas, his children gone:
one in reform school
moved on to prison,
two others never wrote.

For thirty years he's lived
on insulin. His diabetic legs,
gangrened, have been severed
above the ankles,
above the knees.
His eyesight's failed.
From a wheelchair he raises
gardens every spring,
sometimes sticks in mud
and falls, lies calling
Help, and crying. Always
someone has come. He phones
my mother once a month,
weeps for his boys, weeps How
can I make it up? *There*
there, she says,
not knowing how.

World War I Soldiers,

Louisville, Kentucky,
date unknown: photograph
in a library book.
They march downtown
along the trolley lines

under signs, "Ullman's Ready to Wear"
and "Sterne's Grocery."
They are thin. Their hats are peaked,
their leggings tight.
They carry rifles.

They aren't even nearly
in step. They seem thirty
or older. Their officers march
stiff as boy scouts.
I search the faces for father.

My eyes rake each platoon,
return to one man
in the second rank,
his face dark, only a slash
of light on his cheek and chin.

He is tall. His head is turned.
He is looking through the camera.
Could it be? If he had died
in Flanders, who would have seen
this man I see,

who would have cared?
I stare at the others.
Each one marches alone.

What Old Pilots Say

They say three things do you no good:
altitude above you,
runway behind,
airspeed you haven't got.

Say your engine explodes
on take-off, catches fire,
or simply fails. For seconds
there's a point
of no return: too low to eject
and live, too slow
to bend the bird around
and land.

On final approach
(gear down, flaps extended,
only knots above a stall)
airspeed you don't have
won't help. This phase
they call The Widow-Maker:
a flame-out here
means that you die.

They say any landing
you walk away from
is good.

The Winter Before the War

In fall we raked
the leaves downhill
in heaps high
as the fence,
set them afire
and watched them
burn. In hours
the fire died down,
the mounds of leaves
only a smudge
of black.

Weeks later
the first snow fell.
Weeks after that
the lake one-hundred
yards away was solid,
white, the ice so thick
trucks drove on it.
Fishermen wrapped up like bears
chopped through the ice,
let down their hooks
and waited. Their breaths
resembled chimney smoke.
We pulled the sled
across the lake,
our children
bundled up
and eating snow.

The fireplace
after dark
was where we thawed.
Chocolate steamed
in mugs we wrapped
our hands around.
Our children slept.
The news came on.
We watched
each other's eyes.

Taking Aim

Stalking through jungles
this is the way
you hold your M-16,

muzzle down,
sniffing
like a hundred-dollar dog.

Keep it on automatic.
Anything moves in the bushes,
you open fire:

this damn '16
will rise for you
and point the bastard out.

Kind of pull it sideways,
like this.
Don't aim the damn thing:

point it.
And don't forget: just a touch
on the trigger.

If you're holding it
like this
it'll get him.

Measuring Time

First Granny died. I was
ahead of the batter
and waiting on the mound.
Then I saw Mother
weeping at the door.
I have never
thrown the same way since.

My brother Warren
went away to war.
In junior high
John shot himself.
Terrell burned alive,
trapped in his car.
Then Vietnam:

Stewart nosed in
from twenty-thousand feet,
Fred crashed in flames
outside Hanoi, and Murray
exploded in mid-air
over the green
jungles of the North.
The hands go around, around.

Al Croom

saw a man sliced
to the bone by glass
when a rocket exploded
at Da Nang. Whenever
he told it he laughed.

Croom was nearly seven feet,
his Vietnamese wife
five-three.
When they said goodbye
for his second tour in 'Nam

she wept.
What he did,
sure he would die,
was grin.
Back at Da Nang

when rockets hit
and all of us
crawled under beds
or fled to bunkers,
Croom went walking,

daring the Russian
rockets
to do him in.
I think he wanted
to get it over.

When they shipped him home
it took triple straps
to bind him.
They treated him
for months.

His wife wrote every day.
He sometimes answered her.
Two days before they planned
to mark him fit
for duty

he disappeared,
escaping
whoever still wanted
his head and balls.
I heard weeks later

his doll-like wife
was gone,
no trace of either one.
Al, buddy, it's over,
it's okay.

Veteran

I get as far as the park
this time.
Spectators queer as animals
circle me like a campfire.
They hope I'll fall.

Leaves lie in the park
like tiny bombs
ready to explode. Someday
someone raking
will strike a fuse.
We'll all be killed.

My stumps itch
inside their legs,
lightweight aluminum
clump clump. One of my arms
goes out of control, shifts smoothly
like a transmission, salutes.

They think I'm
shooting a bone
at them. I'm trying
to turn back. They're closing in,
this is Da Nang, their eyes
rake me like AK-47's.

Something of Me Reminds You of Fog

Remember your first night solo
in a jet? Circling San Antonio
in winter, waiting your turn
to be called down. Remember
how the canopy fogged up when finally
you penetrated warmer air
from thirty thousand feet? Forgot
to turn the defroster on. How, ashamed
to admit a mistake, hardly able to see,
you took a chance and landed anyway,
striking the runway hard, too fast,
nose-wheel first, and almost
crashed. Remember your wide eyes
burning? That was I, kissing
your eyeballs, sitting on your lap
lighter than fog. All night
I nibbled your ear, lay soft between
your arms. Did things. You dreamed
of me. At dawn did not remember me
at all. Sometimes you almost
think of my soft touch and secrets
I taught you that good night.
I confess I have slept with others
since. But I have kept my figure.
My breath is still the same.
It will all come back to you
someday. I have your new address.

III

We Three

A blind beggar with pinned-up
khaki for legs holds a spittoon.
I hesitate, drop in a buck,
take one of the pencils. Put it back.

One of the two beside me goes through
elaborate parodies in mime—
stoops, fingers a bill into
an imaginary cup, pats an imaginary

beggar on the head, walks toward me
with eyes rolled up toward heaven,
hands together in blessedness.
Breaks into silent laughter, breaks wind,

pointing at me. He slaps his knee
and holds his sides. He is
the harlequin, white splotches
on his eyelids, cheeks and chin.

Makes fun of everything I do.
The other merely scowls.
Drags his heels and scowls,
fists crammed in his tight pockets.

Makes me feel nothing's worth
living for. The clown prances along
behind, gooses me sometimes. I swing
at him. He skips away and laughs.

The White-Haired
Trial Judge Deliberates

The books, yes all the books
are here, shelved like anchovies
along my chamber walls,
canned applications of the laws.
My thumbs with clean blunt nails
know how to open
and shut a case. It is not
precedent I need. I know
what to do. They call me
Bulldog Thurmond: I cling
to a case until I find its jugular.
I know what I would rule
were I the appellate judge:
sustain the trial judge.
There is no doubt. The prosecution
has draped its burden of proof
down around my shoulders
like a robe. I know
the word to say.
For a minute more
my lips are sealed. Saying it
is the human arrogance,
is why they cry Your Honor.

The Lifeguard

She is squeezing your chest with the smallest
hands. You imagine that her bikini top
sags open and you can see everything.
Tilting your head back
she begins to kiss you deep,
her warm legs touching your arm.
You are dying with pleasure.
She stops kissing each time you try
to respond. Your lungs slosh
as she massages your chest.
Again she kisses you,
her mouth sideways to yours, but sensuous.
When you want her to go on forever,
she stops, rolls your eyelids closed.
You begin to freeze.

Snow Takes Us

Snow takes us down to the station.
We wait until the train comes in
rumbling over the rails like hunger.
Newsboys go by, hawking the latest griefs.
The price of news, we notice, has gone up.

Pigeons huddle under the eaves of buildings
like snowballs solid as brass.
From the engine nothing comes, not even steam.
No one we know steps from the train.
Hello, hello, they do not say.

With only luggage they slip into cabs
and crunch down avenues inches deep.
People who look like friends we used to know
rush aboard. The doors close.
The train grinds away.

Last Words to an
Apprentice Undertaker

Remember, you can't be yourself,
you are somebody else, you are
nobody. All you are there for
is to get it done.
The relatives will do the rest,
the twisted faces, the tears,
the final recognition that someone
is really there, inside the coffin.
Their friends will play the chorus,
ready to say their lines
at the proper time. You merely
pull the strings, pausing
to let each person play his role.

If there are no friends,
you should act concerned,
standing near the family
like a distant cousin.

If there is no one
except the widow, stand closer by.
Get ready to support her if she falls.
If she turns to you, weeping,
put on your soft voice and say
there there, there there.

When there is not even a widow,
you may be yourself.

The Buried

Out in a field of statues and stones
and graveled roads that intersect
like checkerboards, under their leveled sod
the bodies lie. They bend their
cramped backs and stiffen to escape.
Their hands feel numb, feel tied with cords.
Their mouths seem gagged; their muffled screams,
like wind swirling past marble.
Horizontally the pleas are heard:
they're not alone. On every side each hears
the others. They strain to kick, to turn,
to tunnel out, to reach each other.

They know their souls kneel overhead,
collapsed, face down and sobbing,
unable to help. The bodies one by one
lie back to rest, and one by one
they sleep. Years go by. The souls lie still
with ears pressed to the earth.
Sometimes they hear bones click as loved ones
shift in sleep. And one by one
the souls curl up in slabs of stone
and clutch what once were knees.

IV

Oases

Counting the moon, at least five remain. Elk, though you seldom see them, still roam the high country. If you were born lucky and hike for days without guns or food, you can sometimes hear them bugling in the fall.

At night, on beaver walks farther downstream, shivering, if you hear the stream sighing you can aim your lantern and might pierce the plastered hair, the eyes like anthracite, before the broad tail slaps the water and is gone.

Or you could even on the prairie find a cave somewhere. You need not die of thirst. Be aware of bees: if you find a wet one mark a line toward its home. There, behind a waterfall below ground level, deafened by the roar inside the cave where thousands of bees swarm, rest, don't even move, and hearing nothing but the roar of gallons of wings, drink only the mind's slow honey and lick yourself clean of thirst.

Or if you can abide guano and the eternal fluttering of bats returning like rowdy bastards at dawn, the whirr of millions of mosquitoes dying in bat bellies pendant from the ceiling; and if you do not fear the ceiling might slowly close down upon you, stalactites descending nearer drip by drip, then you might go down with tons of candles into the caverns, the deeper caves, and begin again.

Going Home

From forty-thousand feet the earth
is a dead planet. Scratches like cuniform
show some race once tried existing there.
We recognize roads that are thin lines
erratic as the canals on Mars,
and patterns like printed circuitry
which we know are towns.

Lakes like amoebas as we pass by
turn bright, turn solid, glare hard
like glaciers. Nothing looks polluted,
guarded by shotguns or barbed wire,
nothing seems threatened or afraid.
Far off on the horizon puffs of clouds
hover like gunfire. It is not our war.

We realize cars we cannot see
careen faster than legal limits
on those lines, but if they should crash
and all die screaming
we could not notice.
Passing through clouds
we watch the earth disappear.

The clouds grow thick, our world confined
from here out to the wings,
even the tips vague in a blaze of white.
Buffeting begins. The cabin creaks and jerks
and hostesses hold on, balancing their trays
like our precarious lives. Suddenly
we drop, hundreds of feet.

Seatbelts bind our legs. Drinks spill.
The aircraft bangs and lurches
in a climb. Hostesses lift themselves,
smile grimly, their knuckles white
as they distribute napkins.
Their hands reaching out
jerk in the aisle like puppets.

We watch the wings bend.
Hostesses hobble to the stern,
strap in. It seems
we hear rivets popping.
Near the front a child cries.
It seems we hear
the mother crying, too.

The earth, we confess throughout our
shaken bodies, is still our home,
a globe of graveyards and crashed planes.
When we descend, the clouds thin out
and there it sprawls,
the rock on which we live
and where we all return.

Never in My Life

had I heard my father mention
love. By twelve I felt something
missing, a girlfriend, or millions
of rabbits I needed to murder.
By twenty I knew, but told myself
it did not matter. I had never told him,

either. By thirty, after years
of emergencies and two children,
I admitted to myself it did.
By forty, after a war and another child,
I resolved before we died
we would say it.
I returned from Southeast Asia

to hold my wife, each child,
to bless or to be blessed by father.
We shook hands. Months passed
the same. One night they rushed him
to the hospital. Drugged, for days
he lived by shots and tubes.
The night his hands moved

I lingered in the room,
the nurse waiting with crossed arms
while I studied this man
who fought in Flanders.
Bending down
louder than I meant
I called his name.

The dim eyes opened,
tried focusing
without glasses.
Up past the failing heart,
he mumbled Humm?
I touched the blue vein
of our blood that throbbed

beneath his head's pale skin, slowly,
slowly pulsing. I brushed his sparse
white wisps of hair back into place,
held my hand on his cool skull
and spoke the words.
His breathing stopped.
I thought *I've killed him.*

At last his dry lips closed.
He breathed again. Somewhere
far back of the blur in his eyes
I imagined electrons flashing,
decoding this dim disturbing news
for his numbed brain.
Squinting, his eyes sank far away,

away from me and from the ceiling,
down maybe to his childhood
and his own dead father's doors.
The empty eyes jerked back
and focused on my face.
Fiercely I focused too
and kept the contact tight.

Then the drugs drowned him again
in sleep. It was enough,
was all I could receive or ever give
to him. Even in that glaze
that stared toward death,
I had seen him take me in,
been blessed by what I needed all my life.

Evolution

Wisteria tendrils
bounce about in the wind.

Think of the speed of sunlight
lasering the leaves,
lengthening the headless
tendrils that grow more slowly

than mud snails sucking their way
up the wall. Come back
in a week: out of all angles
of possible growth, some
have wound around twigs,

around wrought iron grillwork,
over piton-edges of the bricks.
What vegetable intelligence:
the speed of light
slowed to this creeping photosynthesis,
knowing somehow where to go.

Passing By

Black land plowed
furrow-deep, the ridges
rounded by more than
one season's rain, fallow,
ready to re-plow and plant.
Ahead, the farmhouse is almost
reclaimed by trees, no paint,
black tractor on blocks,
For Sale sign faded,
in the yard the plows,
the rusted harrow,
a child's tire hung
on a frayed rope, windows
of the farmhouse smashed,
the culvert to the drive
collapsed.
On down the road
a farmer on a red machine
plows plumes of dust
ten rows at a time.

Weekends

In the evening,
snails that started up at dawn
have reached the windowsills.

Across the road
my neighbor's bellwether
begins his waddle
to the barn.

Mule deer,
ears everywhere,
step out into the grain
and start to graze.

The porch swing shuttles
back and forth
and I smell rain:
east of the ranch
dark thunderheads boil pink.

I drag my feet, the swing
stops. My hand
reaches for the dog.

With Steve at Lake Raven

The snakes this time of day would all be basking
on the bank, I tell him, curled around some driftwood
dreaming of rodents. Come in, the water's fine.

My six-year-old steps back and takes a breath,
comes running to the water with a splash, swims out
and grabs my neck. His black hair shines,

and treading water I feel him trembling, his body
warm still from the sun. Bobbing in the lake
he starts to laugh. Race you out there,

he says, small finger pointing at the buoy.
I let him launch away, his feet against my chest,
and follow in his wake. The sun breaks bright

at every breath, the lake not clear, but flashing
like reflectors, burning holes in my eyes.
I pause, tread water, and squinting find Steve

almost to the buoy. He swims in an arc toward it,
the long way there. His thin strong arms
chop through waves as another boat speeds by.

I ride the first wave and start again,
keeping him in sight through slitted eyes.
He scrambles up the tapered marker

and hangs on as it tilts, his victory cry
ringing like a sea bell. I swim there
and let myself sink under, bob back above the surface

and reach to touch his shining hair, sway with him
as the buoy sways, laugh with my son
and think no matter, we are together now.

The End of Summer

At night, camped by the lake,
we hear our son's soprano laugh,
his brother's baritone, the thump of oars
and swish of water sliced:
one more row across Lake Raven,
moonlight a sheet of silver
where they go, laughing at nothing,
laughing at everything. Next week,
Carl leaves for college, Steve enters
second grade. The canoe will be
lashed inverted in the yard.
Spiders will be spinning there.

Sangre de Cristo,
September 6:
the Holy Mountain

Listen: the snap
you heard may break
again. No one is near.

Thin pine-air
chills your blood,
the blood of Christ magenta
on the raw mountains,

the late sun cool
as a deer's nose. Snap.
No one is near.

Shift your pack higher
and climb,
steep now, the weight
on your back like wings
that will not spread.

Cougar or deer,
whatever it was,
has slipped behind.

Hours. Rocks roll downhill,
cushioned in nets
of green. Finally
you see:

the cross of snow
in mountain crevasses,
in shadow, lies
like blue light.

Burning the Fence

The kindling curls
and greys out, crackles
and drops through the grating.

Flames pale as rust
tack themselves to posts
brittle as old bones
and waver within cracks.

Clenched tight, the posts
hold in their flames,
unwilling to stop being fence.

Bermuda Grass

Root-rot and winter kill,
still the old grass comes back,
cracks in the drive and sidewalk
caulked with green, pale blades
spading up under layers of weeds
and leaves crumbling to mulch, Bermuda
rooting runners everywhere in connected
directionless sprawl, all going to seed
breeding in the wind, scattering the lawn
with spawn like dragons' teeth that eat
peat moss or sand and grow, that not drought,
sprouting weeds, root-rot nor winter kills.